Postcards from the Dead Letter Office

tanka
and other
poems

Dawn Manning

Postcards
from the
Dead Letter Office

Copyright © 2016 by Dawn Manning
All rights reserved

This is a work of poetry. Names, characters, businesses, places, events and incidents are either the products of the author's imagination or used in a fictitious manner. Any resemblance to actual persons, living or dead, or actual events is purely coincidental.

Published by Burlesque Press
www.burlesquepressllc.com

ISBN: 978-0-9964850-3-6

Book design by Daniel Wallace

Cover art by Andrea Tan

Image of Venice by Jörg Bittner (Unna)
shared with a Creative Commons Attribution-Share Alike 3.0 Unported license.

for Scott,
who wanders with me

Table of Contents

Introduction	1
Topophilia	3
[borderlands tanka]	4
First Ocean	6
[Mexico tanka]	7
Hit, Run	11
[spring tanka]	12
The Mummy's Cherita	16
[Tyrolean tanka]	17
Dead Letters I	21
[Venetian tanka]	22
Oculus	25
[summer tanka]	26
State of the Union	31
[Amazon tanka]	32
Fall, Fly: A Mirror Tanka	36
[Andean tanka]	37
Dead Letters II	40
[autumn tanka]	41
Monet's Poplars on the Epte	46
[museum tanka]	47
Oranges in Winter	50
[Scotland tanka]	51
O Tannenbaum	54
[winter tanka]	55
Dead Letters III	58
[China tanka]	59
Night Watch	62
[Hong Kong tanka]	63
Notes	66

Introduction

I wrote my first tanka by accident. I had five short lines that centered on one image shifting into another and I had begun poking around the internet for short verse forms that might point me in a direction I could take it. I discovered cinquains, and though I've used cinquain forms several times in this book, this particular poem marched to a different beat. The closest poetic tradition I knew that resembled my little poem was a haiku—a haiku with a person in it. And as tangent gave way to tangent in my internet browser, I discovered this semi-feral creature of a poem called tanka.

Tanka is a form of Japanese lyric poetry with a history that stretches back more than 1300 years. Traditionally these 'short songs' consisted of five unrhymed phrases broken into a pattern of 5-7-5-7-7 sound units (*on*).

For tanka in English, counting sound units would create poems that are too short (as a word like 'Tokyo' contains only two syllables, but four *on*), so many writers of English language tanka count syllables instead, thus arranging tanka into five lines of 5-7-5-7-7 syllables. 31 English syllables, however, can feel long, so it is more accurate to think of a tanka as a five-line poem that can be said in about two breaths (with the minimalists tending towards tanka of one breath and the prolific tending towards tanka of three breaths).

What's most important is the irregular but distinct rhythm, and the relationship of form and content to create tension and/or a pivot. This is often achieved by the juxtaposition of images, an image and a response, or the movement from strophe to antistrophe. Other techniques central to tanka include the use of the objective correlative, *volta* (or turn, in which the poem feels suspended and a new idea is introduced), and *zeugma* (in which the middle line completes the thought or image of the first component, but can also be read as the first line of the second component).

Though tanka can be arranged in thematic sets as I've done here, each tanka is meant to stand alone as an aesthetic whole.

Individual tanka do not have titles, do not begin with capitalization, and do not end with punctuation to keep the form open. They rely on simple diction, and the use of clear, intense images to convey emotion.

I've employed the use of all of these elements in composing tanka at one time or another, including the *kyoka*, or 'mad poem' in which satire and the acerbic are favored over the lyric, and the poet takes on the role of both the observer and the observed. There are no subjects off limits, making tanka a form as flexible or rigid as a writer wishes it to be.

    cadence wades waist deep
    through the river
    of an image,
    shifts midstream
    into fields of wildflowers

Dawn Manning
Lansdowne, PA
December 2015

Topophilia

I'm always crossing horizons I once believed in,
boundaries not as solid as the borders
these scratched tracks mapped
into white space pretend. There's always a way across—

one place longs for another—asphalt
dreams gravel, gravel dreams dirt,
and we all dream water. We
are always becoming. This is the wanderer

and the poem, blackened feet sticking out at right angles,
silhouettes like skeleton keys. And
having keys, we look
for what they open; having feet, we make roads.

[borderlands tanka]

on Sundays
brass collection plates
usher in
new galaxies of silver
and copper suns

                         I won't read this old church book,
                         but keep it close—the cover
                         flipped open
                         to the blocky cursive
                         of your name

luck, lies,
and longing
fold their hands
in prayer
all their fingers crossed

last straws, camel-needles—
makings of that little pig's
flimsy house—but
they'll get us through the night if
that's all we have to work with

> *you needed the scars,*
> *the years in the desert,*
> whispers the muse,
> *the way fire needs darkness,*
> *something to devour*

all myths root in fear
and sorrow, all heroes
unravel the blue threads
of their wrists to staunch
the bleeding of another

First Ocean

We scale
dunes in darkness
at Puerto Peñasco
that Spring Break, our light dissolving
in the
great, black
sound: the sea sucking the land out
from under us, the world
slowly swallowed
by sea.

[Mexico tanka]

friendship rings
somersault through
Pacific waves,
the tide's magnetic pole
driving us apart

                          we carve our hearts
                          in the old bridge
                          so that anyone crossing
                          the river knows
                          what anchored there

jacaranda limbs sway
by the techno club's
bass-thumped
stucco walls—
spring mating dance

tone-deaf
on even-numbered pages
of bilingual works—
where did I learn to split
avocados with my tongue?

                         tarnished *milagros*
                         litter altars
                         fish, corn, limbs, hearts
                         tin rain
                         in a time of drought

in the sun-scorched plaza
wondering at our life
in this world,
an ant rests
in my high-noon shadow

he's just bleached bones
in the desert now,
but coyotes
still can't wipe the smile
from that old mule's skull

                    under the pink lights
                    of the *parroquia*
                    she splits her heart open—
                    geode brighter than
                    the jewelry vender's wares

papel picado makers
lace skulls with the songbirds
of small chisels—
our delicate chitchat
shaped by what we leave out

poorly translating
Spanish poems—at the window
"mariposa!"
flits with ease from
the chrysalis of my tongue

Hit, Run

The husk
of the orange tabby

seeps between the seams
of the earth a little each day,

a white picket
stuck down her throat to lob her

into the irrigation ditch,
stuck so deep it dislodged six half-circles

curled in her belly.
We keep vigil from our bicycles

as life scurries back into the cat,
ant by ant.

[spring tanka]

ultrasound
unfolds limbs
from heartbeats, my niece
a cricket
in an origami box

                                    even newborns know
                                    their fists must break
                                    into petals, the husks
                                    of their eyes must split open
                                    to pull in the world

crocuses knife through
the chipped paint of frost—
I too resurrect
memory's green patina
by force

I staple my heart
to telephone poles
on Good Friday; soon
I will compose another
pathetic cat poem

        spring winds sweep goslings
        like loose lint
        from under their mother's
        downy skirt—I only
        throw out most of your old things

shifting books
from here to there,
stirring up dust—
when I pray to forgive
what I mean is forget

neighbors look up
from tulip beds as the sun
peeks over roofs—
brazed faces blossom
from within straw-petaled hats

                            t'ai chi masters weave limbs
                            between bystanders—
                            in the sycamore's shadow
                            spiders knit doilies
                            cross-stitched with corpses

heat swells the chrysalis,
vents stratus clouds of silk—
a hundred citron raindrops
hit soil and bounce off
on mantis legs

walking between
grave rows,
zipper teeth
join earth
to heaven

                          robins at Grandma's grave,
                          too busy building
                          nests of silk flowers
                          and cigarettes
                          for sermons on heaven

The Mummy's Cherita

Ötzi's barred tattoos keep tally—

how the body goes on alone
in the dark. For a Euro I press

his silhouette into a souvenir coin—
an artifact of an artifact
to help me count the costs.

[Tyrolean tanka]

only the guard dog knows
if it's the fingers of fog
or the poems
that rebuild Brunnenburg
each morning stone by stone

                                  dawn bezels the Alps
                                  in light, swifts fall ash-soft
                                  from the bright ridge—
                                  black stars smoldering
                                  in the peach orchard

cable cars scurry
up single-strand webs—
even from this height I see
our shadows remain
in the Adige Valley

I lost the knell and bleat
of the goat path,
felt my way along
a braille of edelweiss
to the rock face of a canto

                              carved nativities
                              for sale by Alpine trails,
                              wise men in lederhosen
                              pass by Saviors
                              of fine German craftsmanship

at harvest
cornstalks stake
the Savior's hands—
Christ crucified
by an older god

bees honeycomb
the tunnels mice gnaw through six
centuries of wood;
the walls hum Ezra's tune,
make it new! make it new!

                what bruise in the eye
                of the golden-haired girl
                in the painting still tends
                to tea and her father's
                spine-snapped books years later?

fog folds and unfolds
this thin mountain air—
your letters creased again
into the pockets
of my way-stopped heart

in summer we threw peaches
into the sun; by autumn
over-ripe tumors
break the branches
of my empty womb

                                      the kitchen's still bright
                                      with wine and singing,
                                      without a torch I walk
                                      over the mountains
                                      and into the stars

Dead Letters I

Thin
victories,
breath absorbed in white-
space, blue straits feed and fed by
ink,
years,
the hole-punched aorta's pulp
pulse—red dispatch of
my paper
heart.

[Venetian tanka]

moored gondolas
saddled by monochrome men—
new moons
drowning their hearts
in what they mistake for sky

                              the Lacemaker's hands
                              flounder at the sides of her
                              crocheted dress—
                              without pockets there's no net
                              to quiet these gasping fish

pastel laundry
strung between windowsills—
prayer flags and flypaper
for photographers
on the tourist's pilgrimage

these scattered isles—
chicken bones divined
with the soles of our feet—
our quarrels with the future
solved by tossing out our map

                  how ridiculous—
                  a ring of Murano glass!
                  I wear it anyway,
                  knowing you'll flutter to
                  anything that gives off light

we feel our way through
cathedral ribs arched along
canals like beached whales,
each one of us a Jonah
seeking out a second chance

broken seeds of light rain down
from Mother Mary's halo—
on the ledge below
mosaic heavens
hatchlings tilt open their throats

                        islands sag beneath
                        gelato-touting tourists;
                        there are no Venetians
                        in Venice, but even
                        Keith Richards ate here once

Oculus

Headlights
reveal the chase
in two flashes: the deer
runs for its life, but so does
the wolf.

[summer tanka]

we wake from weak winters
to summer nights trellised
with mock frost: a thousand slugs
scale our house,
teaching us to love the cold

                this fence
                won't see another June—
                nimble-fingered morning glories
                pick off the last layer
                of wrought-iron birch

birds quarrel
with the songs
of garbage trucks—
I wake
to the battle of the bands

the gutted engine
behind the mechanic's shop
hums to life in the rain—
a puddle of kittens
marooned in the split muffler

                    repair manuals
                    and doctor bills interlock
                    on the kitchen table—
                    lettuce leaves petaled tight
                    around my scrap-paper poems

endometriosis,
fibromyalgia—
saxifrages break the rock
of my body open
from the inside out

toasting another year,
our napkins flutter down
from the rooftop restaurant—
crumpled doves
swoop between high-rises

                grey head bowed
                he mows lawns, patches cement—
                any work that keeps the lights on
                at home
                his ailing wife

grey head bowed
he limps past my failed garden
with gifts of zucchini
and tomatoes—
Christmas in July

plastic flower barrettes
swing from braided stems—
a garden blooms
from the dark soil
of her mind

                          startled by the nursing fox
                          shed of her coat
                          I drop the chicken leg,
                          she snatches it up:
                          a fair exchange rate

I text my clutch
of small poems,
you huddle in a stairwell—
between us
a tornado touches down

the thrill of flashlight tag
at dusk—
fireflies float
from flowerbeds
charting new constellations

                              twilight crickets om
                              the sound of zero;
                              each beauty
                              only lasts a season or
                              we'd never let go

State of the Union

A wilderness
travels through me,

lean and savage
as Spanish moss—

bromeliads,
and strangler vines—

the body a
language star-crossed.

[*Amazon tanka*]

blue-green-red-gold parrots
squawk and scrape
clay cliff walls—at sunrise
all our squabbles
clamor hope

                    open-walled lodge,
                    traditional thatched roof:
                    the mortar and pestle
                    stand still at the center
                    of the buffet breakfast room

morning traffic jam,
capuchins cross our trail
on low-slung vines—
the frowning alpha
urinates at my feet

dehydrated, we climb
the platform anyway—
dead trees
spider vein white
above the canopy

                        how long did I halt fearing
                        the watcher in the river—
                        this meek capybara
                        hiding from
                        the predator on my shore

the Russian in gold chains
plucks a piranha
from the oxbow lake,
shows me his yellow belly
beneath razor teeth

young Ese'eja guides
tend the medicine garden
with broken English
they split thorned seed pods
smear red on their lips

                              the shaman blares Shakira
                              from the bar he tends by day,
                              hums the tune of tree frogs
                              as he heals twisted ankles
                              by candlelight

at dusk I stick to rivers—
each time the sun sets
behind trees, it rises
through water into
the dark clouds of distant shores

night fills with a grim clawing,
I peek out
of my mosquito nets:
mouse gnawing through my bag
to feast on plantain chips

Fall, Fly: A Mirror Tanka

        eye level with a condor   falling into flying
        ten thousand feet up,   I call you—
                  bear witness   through the static
                to the shriek   from both our throttled throats
the condor-clutched pigeon   all my bad decisions

[Andean tanka]

tourists line the upper walls,
look down on the sunrise
at Machu Picchu;
each stone below tilts
to linger in the light

                    dawn first gilds
                    the Temple of the Sun
                    silver and gold
                    beaming in the corner
                    broom and dustpan

the Inca mapped and named
the dark clouds
between stars—
tapestry
now moth-eaten by flashbulbs

vista after vista
wind rushes through
the dark caves of our bodies—
my whole faith
a land made mostly of sky

                        altitude sickness,
                        a pack of starved dogs
                        trembles through the alleys
                        of my fevered bones,
                        picking clean my homesick spine

when did it become
too much trouble
to retrieve dropped pennies?
tumbling from a worn pocket
old dreams plink on cobblestones

kneeling in the gutter
I salvage a scrapped poem
scribbled on an old receipt—
it's worth built on the shrine
of my bruised knees

                        nuns chanting in the cloisters
                        of Arequipa—
                        oysters shelled up
                        give their lives
                        for one warped pearl

Dead Letters II

I slip
into the heat
of your body sloughed off
in suburban sheets, draw warmth through
coiled limbs,
and keep
watch over darkened windowpanes
for the ghost of scratched glass
made visible
by rain.

[autumn tanka]

bleating geese vee south—
my neighbor's mourning
is a sound shaped
sharp as a spear,
blunt as a valley

                    at the memorial
                    your shadow reaches me first—
                    another wound
                    grazed by maple leaves,
                    stretched thin and tight

raindrops
swarm in sideways—
a school of silverfish
eating their way through
autumn's amber tapestries

the hurricane grapples
with the great sycamore—
tree all hands, wind all voice—
only shadows speak
fluently with both

                                between storms, candlelight
                                blinks back from your eyes—
                                long-dead stars revealed
                                by overdue conversation,
                                downed power lines

the maple's maroon fire
has gone out—how clearly
I see now
the beautiful, stark tangle
of what we planted then

Christmas catalogs
come so early—
fat squirrels wriggle open
the mailbox to bury nuts
in this pile of dead leaves

                    we keep Halloween vigil
                    with albino toms
                    ghosting through our alley—
                    heat-thin, flame-quick ferals
                    untroubled by their snipped wicks

the wild turkey entourage
bobs, clucks, and gobbles
through the labyrinth
of purring cars—
rush-hour delay no one minds

a warped water ring
peels off the table
with the mug you set aside
hours before, so sure
I'd be here to clear things up

                      autumn's breath
                      lifts my first
                      gray hairs,
                      a candle
                      just blown out

Princess Nukata—I too
wait for someone not coming
as autumn's breeze stirs
the bamboo blinds
we picked out at Target

lay down your sugar-rimmed skull
in my empty bed,
my moon—my
moth-eaten flame, my
cracked song of frost

Monet's Poplars on the Epte

Before X-rays and Rorschach, there was the horizon, water
doubling a stand of poplars into the head
of a reclining Buddha,
into the radioactive glow of a pelvic scan,
stippled green ilium breaking apart
atom from atom

until the landscape
is a death mask, sky filling the hollows
of eyes and muzzle. This shore's not a temple.
It is for sale. Anyone
with thirty pounds can buy a piece of it, harrow
the trees out by their roots, see behind the mask to death itself.

[museum tanka]

I could sit for hours
staring into Van Gogh's sun
translating words
by the thousands
into chips of light

                    his olive trees translate
                    light with bruised tongues—
                    whisper long mosaic shadows
                    into one eye, pull choppy
                    rivers from the other

after Gauguin split,
Van Gogh put galaxies
between himself and the sun,
one of many stars
eclipsed by distance

he walked back to town alone
through his crow-dirged fields,
bullet reached his spine—
how often in dreams I've crossed
wheat fields under troubled skies

                I've never reached Rouen, yet
                I've seen Monet
                resurrect and set the sun
                at its doorstep
                hourly

Renoir's an easy trick—
paint it exact, then
smear the lens of your eye
with Vaseline
and never blink

the hard work's Cézanne's:
chisel sharp-edged light
from soft landscapes, each leaf
perching in the mind
heavy as stone

                                  Cézanne was right—
                                  I can't hear you through
                                  the tangle
                                  of triangles clanging
                                  between the branches

Oranges in Winter

> *For I have known them all already, known them all—*
> *Have known the evenings, mornings, afternoons,*
> *I have measured out my life with coffee spoons…*
> —*T.S. Eliot*

Cigars, cups of tea, trips to
video stores—we kill time in stacks

of used books, omit sound
with scribbled sticky notes, smother

cabin fever with spaghetti dinners;
and we carry bitterness

in our skins like the Clementines
we peel together, carefully

pulling up the veins
with the rind.

[Scotland tanka]

Wallace's tower breaches
the forest canopy—
wind whistling
through the windows
of its leviathan gills

                        eyes on the ground when the sun
                        makes a rare appearance—
                        suddenly a shadow
                        of swooping swallows
                        lays a garland at my feet

circling over the altar
through the stained-glass saints
the ghost
of the caretaker's hand
wipes grime from halos

sunless days, sleepless nights—
the flip-and-flicker
of electronic pages
in my lap
moonlight

                              you reach for me
                              in this many-fingered hand
                              of standing stones
                              just wide enough
                              to hold the sky

how many cups
of tea can we drink
in one day?
embers we horde,
nostalgic for the sun

on the horizon
archaeologists haul stones
through Orkney fog—carefully
I roll my bag down the lane
between want and need

                        heather and moss
                        on the stones
                        of Culloden Moor—
                        scar tissue spindles fingers
                        into the smallest cracks

pebbles still wedged
in my boot-soles
I walk out of the
Philadelphia airport
on Scottish isles

O Tannenbaum
for Grandpa Breid

He who hardly spares a word
but for the weather, found the German
left in his tongue, and sang over the static
of ships filled with Midwest farm boys,
over the wails of Japanese mothers
burrowed into hills to warm
the naked atoms of their children; he sang
between barren mountains of bicycles
blistered thousands high, trees felled
under human snow.

[winter tanka]

winter hungers
for heat stored in skin,
bites with crystal barbs,
the even gnaw
of saw-toothed habits

                semitrucks shed
                snow skins along the highway—
                our skittish sedan
                a mouse darting through
                a migration of snakes

huddled in a knitting circle
the copse of trees
wiles away cold nights
crocheting
scarves of fog

skeins of fog
unspool
across the road—
scarves picked loose
by rush-hour headlights

                        white outs make
                        lumbering meteorites
                        of impatient cars;
                        the lights along the El
                        our guiding constellation

my car-battered arm propped up,
your head on my hip—
the tablet you hold
shines down on the new ways
we find to fit together

we fly over
rime-wrapped packages
of forest and field,
the silver river leading home
a ribbon just pulled loose

                    we burn balsam incense
                    in our drafty row—
                    with the power out
                    and no safe place for fire,
                    our words plume cold smoke

white outs
abridge skylines
to the person
in front of you,
in front of me

Dead Letters III

I drop
the cigar box,
spill your cursive—tangled
fishline that still pulls at my eye;
old phone
cords once ended in the same barbed
hook—your voice coiling in
my ear and my
wet mouth.

[China tanka]

taking the night train
I watch through the window
for village lights—
seeds scattered
in dark soil

                one ripple
                a rumor skims the temple pond,
                ten ripples
                koi surface
                for spring gossip

gridlock of kite-flying,
I trip again on the cracks
in Tiananmen square—
twin boys dressed as Robin,
no Batman in sight

she knelt here on June fourth,
shirt a nest stuffed in
bullet holes; today
her laugh a thousand sparrows
everywhere at once

                              chain-smokers
                              watch me copy quotes into
                              my note book
                              filled with the words of others
                              second hand smoke

no wind to lift our kites
above the dust—
my pale face in the photos
of every passerby
defined by what's missing

why do our questions
end in spilled noodles,
river bends, fish hooks?
a pair of black swans
glides across Heavenly Lake

                                      Milky Way candy bar,
                                      standing room only—
                                      the universe melts
                                      in my pocket
                                      on a Beijing bus

Night Watch

What keeps us upright
if not the moon?

That white knuckle
beckoning—our bodies,

heavy as oceans, salt
washed up on the skin.

[Hong Kong tanka]

jetlagged, I slurp
my host's small bird soup—
what I would be if
I could dream myself out
of this nest of jumbled bones

                                    alone on the rooftop
                                    overlooking the temple
                                    even here
                                    someone plays Chopsticks
                                    in the distance

noodles swirl
shrimp comets, pea globes,
water chestnut moons—
another solar system
blossoms in a steaming wok

he tells me the neon signs
are dying out—ghost
of his bent-glass words haunted
by the ghost of his shaky
calligraphy

                        avoiding eye contact
                        with night market hawkers—
                        what I want
                        not as clear
                        as what I don't want

streets closed for the maids
on their day off—
din of a hundred thousand
trees gilding the wind
with pollen

long distance call, drone
of jackhammers and traffic—
on the other side of the world
my brother turns sixteen,
pierces his ear

                        our foot falls echo
                        through crowded
                        subway tunnels—
                        all we leave unsaid,
                        all we can't unsay

I fill my mind with rain,
map myself in vertical
descents—wild garden
of high-rises, gutters
brimming with plum venders

Notes

"Topophilia"
Topophilia means love of place. This poem was written in conversation with Lynda Hogan's poem "Restless" and contains language from that poem.

[mexico tanka]
The tanka "under the pink lights…" is for C.W. and the *brujas* of San Miguel.

[Tyrolean tanka]
The Tyrol is a unique geographic and cultural landscape that includes the Alpine regions of western Austria and northern Italy. Brunnenburg castle and the Ezra Pound Center for Literature are located in the Italian part known as South Tyrol.
"Make it new" is Pound's famous refrain from *The Cantos*.

[autumn tanka]
The tanka "Princess Nukata—I too…" refers to a tanka by 7th century Japanese poet Nukata no Ōkimi.

"Monet's Poplars on the Epte"
This particular painting from Monet's poplars series is housed in the National Galleries of Scotland. As the poplars were being sold off for timber, a timber merchant helped buy the trees for 30£ so that Monet could continue painting them. The lines "This shore's not a temple. / It is for sale" refers to Ezra Pound's variable incantation in *The Cantos*: "The temple is holy because it is not for sale" (canto 97 and 98).

[museum tanka]
These poems are reflections on both a general knowledge of the artists and their work as well as meditations on specific works of art. The works of art informing this series include: Vincent van Gogh's *Olive Trees* housed in the Minneapolis Institute of Art (MIA), Paul Cézanne's *Chestnut Trees at Jas de Bouffan* (MIA), and the astounding collection of art at The Barnes Foundation in Philadelphia, including works by all of the artists mentioned in this tanka set.

"Oranges in Winter"
The epigraph is from the poem "The Love Song of Alfred J. Prufrock" by T.S. Eliot.

[Scotland tanka]
The tanka "heather and moss…" refers to the site of the Battle of Culloden, the final confrontation in the Jacobite rising of 1745—a battle that still resonates powerfully in the Scottish psyche.

"O Tannenbaum"
The title is the original German name of the song know in English as "O Christmas Tree."

[China tanka]
The tanka "she knelt here on June fourth…" is for *S.* and refers to the Tiananmen Square Massacre.

Acknowledgements

Many thanks to the editors of the following publications where these poems first appeared, sometimes in different versions:

Apiary—"O Tannenbaum"
Atlas Poetica—tanka beginning "moored gondolas," "the Lacemaker's hands," "pastel laundry," " islands sag beneath," "only the guard dog," "cable cars scurry," "dawn bezels the Alps," "the kitchen's still bright," "bees honeycomb," "what bruise in the eye," "fog folds and unfolds," and "walking between"
Burlesque Press Variety Show—"Monet's Poplars" and *[museum tanka]*
The Centrifugal Eye—"Oranges in Winter"
escarp—"Night Watch" and "Oculus"
A Hundred Gourds—tanka beginning "a warped water ring"
Moonbathing—tanka beginning "autumn's breath"
Mudfish—"Hit, Run"
Ribbons—tanka beginning "Milky Way candy bar"

tanka beginning "Milky Way candy bar…" was awarded an honorable mention by the Tanka Society of America through the Sanford Goldstein International Tanka Contest.

The poem "Dead Letters II" appeared in *Poems for the Writing: Prompts for Poets* by Valerie Fox and Lynn Levin (Texture Press, 2013) under the title "The Widow's Cinquains."

* * *

Special thanks to my sharp-eyed, word-wise readers: Shelley Puhak, Kelly McQuain, Scott Manning, Bill Lavender, John Gery, Valerie Fox, Jordan Franklin, Traci Brimhall, and especially to Nate Kostar for seeing the potential for these petite poems in the first place. My deepest gratitude extends to Jeni and Daniel Wallace for guiding me through my many sticky attempts at fitting the universe on a postage stamp.

About the Author

Dawn Manning is a writer, photographer, and rogue anthropologist living in the Greater Philadelphia area. Her awards include the Beullah Rose Poetry Prize, the Edith Garlow Poetry Prize, and the San Miguel Writer's Conference Writing Award, among others. Her poems have been published through *Crab Orchard Review, Fairy Tale Review, Silk Road Review, Smartish Pace, Unsplendid,* and other literary journals.

You can find her online at dawnmanning.com. When the stars align, she travels.

www.ingramcontent.com/pod-product-compliance
Lightning Source LLC
LaVergne TN
LVHW041550070426
835507LV00011B/1019